HMS GLASSHOUSE

Sean O'Brien

Oxford   New York

OXFORD UNIVERSITY PRESS

Oxford University Press, Great Clarendon Street, Oxford OX2 6DP

Oxford New York
Athens Auckland Bangkok Bogota Bombay Buenos Aires
Calcutta Cape Town Dar es Salaam Delhi Florence Hong Kong Istanbul
Karachi Kuala Lumpur Madras Madrid Melbourne Mexico City
Nairobi Paris Singapore Taipei Tokyo Toronto Warsaw

and associated companies in
Berlin Ibadan

Oxford is a trade mark of Oxford University Press

First published in Oxford Poets
as an Oxford University Press paperback 1991
Reprinted in Oxford Poets 1997

British Library Cataloguing in Publication Data
Data available

Library of Congress Cataloging in Publication Data
O'Brien, Sean, 1952–   .
HMS Glasshouse / Sean O'Brien.
p.   cm.—(Oxford poets)
I. Title.   II. Series.
PR6065.B744H58   1991   821'.914—dc20   91–11600
ISBN 0–19–282835–5

Printed in Hong Kong

This book is for Gerry Wardle

ACKNOWLEDGEMENTS

Acknowledgements are due to the editors of the following, in which some of these poems first appeared: *Antaeus*, *Bête Noire*, *Foolscap*, *Gallimaufry*, *High on the Walls: a Morden Tower Anthology* (Bloodaxe Books, 1990), *Jacaranda Review*, *London Magazine*, *London Review of Books*, *The North*, *Observer*, *The Orange Dove of Fiji*, *The Poetry Book Society Anthology 1988–9*, *Radio Three*, *The Rialto*, *Sunk Island Review*, *The Times Literary Supplement*, and *Voices Aloud*.

A number of these poems appeared in pamphlet form as *Boundary Beach* (The Honest Ulsterman, 1989).

The author wishes to thank the Scottish Arts Council and the University of Dundee for the Fellowship in Creative Writing in 1989–91.

CONTENTS

'My memories go back to the time I was six. I remember the railway passing in front of the house and the sea stretching out to the horizon. You sometimes had the impression that the railway came out of the sea or went into it—whichever you like.'

Debussy to Jacques Durand, 24 March 1908

1

BEFORE

Make over the alleys and gardens to birdsong,
The hour of not-for-an-hour. Lie still.
Leave the socks you forgot on the clothesline.
Leave slugs to make free with the pansies.
The jets will give Gatwick a miss
And from here you could feel the springs
Wake by the doorstep and under the precinct
Where now there is nobody frozenly waiting.
This is free time, in the sense that a handbill
Goes cartwheeling over the crossroads
Past stoplights rehearsing in private
And has neither witness nor outcome.
This is before the first bus has been late
Or the knickers sought under the bed
Or the first cigarette undertaken,
Before the first flush and cross word.
Viaducts, tunnels and motorways: still.
The mines and the Japanese sunrise: still.
The high bridges lean out in the wind
On the curve of their pinkening lights,
And the coast is inert as a model.
The wavebands are empty, the mail unimagined
And bacon still wrapped in the freezer
Like evidence aimed to intrigue our successors.
The island is dreamless, its slack-jawed insomniacs
Stunned by the final long shot of the movie,
Its murderers innocent, elsewhere.
The policemen have slipped from their helmets
And money forgets how to count.
In the bowels of Wapping the telephones
Shamelessly rest in their cradles.
The bomb in the conference centre's
A harmless confection of elements
Strapped to a duct like an art installation.
The Première sleeps in her fashion,
Her Majesty, all the princesses, tucked up
With the Bishops, the glueys, the DHSS,
In the People's Republic of Zeds.
And you sleep at my shoulder, the cat at your feet,
And deserve to be spared the irruption

Of if, but and ought, which is why
I declare this an hour of general safety
When even the personal monster—
Example, the Kraken—is dead to the world
Like the deaf submarines with their crewmen
Spark out at their fathomless consoles.
No one has died. There need be no regret,
For we do not exist, and I promise
I shall not wake anyone yet.

THRILLERS AND CHEESE

The night has built a district of its own.
Its residents are killers and the law
And a huddle that might become either.
They stoop at a hatch in the roadside
With lamps, in professional silence,
And choose, it appears, to ignore you.
It happens between the last train and the milk:
The viaduct's dripping with echoes,
The cab-rank deserted, the streetlamps and shadows
As set in their ways as a one-party state
When the rumour of elsewhere has failed.
It is no time of night to be walking,
You say to yourself after too many thrillers
And cheese before bed and bad sleep:
But here you are doing your oral,
Intoning the newsagent, takeaway,
Church of the Dozen True Faithful, then counting
The chairs in the busdrivers' clubroom
Attending a stage from which every last echo
Of Waylon has died, like the humour
You formerly brought to a chance of unease.
You'll say you are out for the smell of the sea
And the paper, for innocent details—
The top copy rutted with string,
The blather of two men up early,
A band of late stars in the fanlight.
But those are no part of this caféless hour,
This death of shebeens, this ticktock
Where urns drip on stairwells,
In which there's no sleep and no moral
And fear has come up like a breath from the drains
With the thought of confession and failure
To know what the crime might have been.
As you stand by the urinous callbox
That waits for emergencies only to stick
A black tongue in your ear, imagine
A rat's nest of sheds at the back of the station,
A man at a desk doing puzzles by striplight,
His life, how it is when he sleeps,
What his notion of honour might be.

He turns from his pastime to make a fresh entry
In infantile biro, and rises and yawns
And goes out for a piss and looks up
At the same constellations, the lights on the line.
He knows what he knows, which is secret,
Constructed, installed and maintained
Without meaning or leave to appeal.
This man you compose in his office,
The shade of subliterate, dutiful evil,
Is one of a mass without number: no telling
Who does or is done to, no circuit to break
And no guilt to award, nor any place
Except inside, where you must know
That thrillers and cheese notwithstanding
You're mad and the whole thing is real.

IN THE OTHER BAR

Forever a winter too old,
With her manners not quite of the moment,
She's wearing it well, the bad sister of London.

For all that the young are pronouncing
On art and safe sex, they will never belong
Where the numberless theatres are dark,

Where the numberless writers have stalled
At the peak of a small reputation
Caressed in damp stacks of *Horizon*,

Which mingles with *Lilliput*, not to deny
The Fitzrovian marriage of letters and smut.
Here the long honeymoon

Waged from Black Rock to the borders of Hove
Will go on so long as a thimble of gin
Can be traced between now and five thirty,

Ensuring the casual entrance of someone
Surprised to be here at this ticklish hour.
Beneath the slow wink of the optic there follows

The search for the chequebook, the novel
To rest on the bar while she smokes
And instructs us that boredom requires

A talent before which the proper responses
Are envy, humility, unbidden refills
And goes-without-saying acceptance

That she makes her entrance once only.
Her friends are the footnotes of footnotes,
Her lovers gone down in the Med

Or the annals of Gordon's, and she
Who has posed and factotumed forever
Could always have been what she chose,

But did not, d'you see, as it happens.
It's almost like love, to be met by a vanity
Nothing corrupts, which is always at home

And has nothing in mind but itself,
The whole lifetime of elegant, objectless
Fucking and fighting, despair as a style

In the district of post-dated cheques
And not-quite prostitution,
Blank beyond judgement and not to be missed.

And when you come back from a pee
She has left you a stool and an ashtray.
Then later when walking through streets

Which can still catch the sun
There is someone who might be an actress
Whose name you can almost remember,

Glimpsed high on a balcony, resting
And staring straight through you
And keeping her looks in this light.

HATRED OF LIBRARIES

So here we are now in the library, wasters.
Scholarship passes its notes to the dead
And the immanent hush of authority damns
Our presumption and jokes and mere presence.

For what in the end are a beer and a sandwich,
A lavatory, someone to meet, if not failures
To grasp what this absolute vault
In the latinate centuries means by itself?

True students are early and warming their hands
At descriptions of hell, and in love
With perpetual winter are glad to be humbled
A lifetime by facts and unbreathable silence:

But we lack the rigour and cannot be still
When the world is refined to a rumour
In draughts, in the sighing of doors which have ceased
To be exits but lead only inwards, to fastnesses

Few may expect to survive and to which we shall
Certainly not be admitted. Through chamber on chamber
The second-rate bones are reduced to a dust
In the lost oubliettes of unwisdom, beyond which

Is waiting that whispered (apocryphal?) work
Which is found in no index and has to be read
With both hands on the table in view of a bishop.
It gives us a laugh. But imagine, O friends

Who have run out of funding and loaf in your sweat
In the guttering days of your final extension,
What might be revealed in that innermost text
To the frivolous hope that within its

Unthinkable pages the Word might yet offer
A light to the desperate. For knowing our sins
And our luck we may fairly suppose
We should find there in black-letter fire: NO SMOKING.

A DONEGAL GOLFER

In my book even golf is sinister,
Played solo at night-time by salesmen
With grudges and one club too many.
Their wall-eyed bull-terriers yawn
In the cars, with the radio on, and I watch.

By the harbour, incendiaries drink
With their in-laws, ambitious morticians
Whose nieces they married and murdered.
These men, do they listen, perhaps, for the tide,
For a torch coming on? I know I do.

At dawn, when the ration of floaters is washed
In the wake of those boats without nets
To which golfers will signal while probing
For oil in the sands of the short seventeenth,
I'm going out. I may be quite some time.

ENTERTAINMENT

In studied southern dialects
By lavatorial viaducts
Threats are passed from hand to hand.
In concrete pillars corpses stand
At permanent attention.

The music slowly claws its way
Through scrublands of conspiracy
Until it finds the keys that mean
The meathook in the ice machine
Beloved of convention.

Verbals or the freezer, lads,
Or residence in riverbeds,
Or something somewhere in between,
The like of which you've never seen,
A startling invention.

The tide comes in. The trains are late.
The night rubs out another date.
The city puts itself to bed
Beside the bagged-up lately dead
Too numerous to mention.

PROPAGANDA

After the whole abandoned stretch,
The bricked-up arches, flooded birchwoods,
The miniature oxbows and dubious schools,
After the B–roads that curved out of sight
Beneath bridges to similar views,
All the scenery hauled away backwards
While this train was heading elsewhere,
After the threat to our faith in the railways,
It seems that at last we have come to the place
That described us before we were thought of.
We stand on its sweltering, porterless platform
And wait in the time-honoured manner.
The stalled afternoon's like a story
Once left on a train with a chapter to go,
Smelling of oil, of dust and old sunlight.
Here are the canopy, flowertubs, posters for war
And the bum-frying torpor of benches.
Here are the smoke in the throat of the tunnel,
The footbridge a guess in the glare, and the clank
As the points irreversibly switch, and here
Is the perfect assurance that somewhere
Close by it is quietly happening.

It's here that Germany in person calls
By parachute, at first confused to death
By Brough and Slough, by classroom spinsters
Jumping on the hand-grenades. Their dull reports
Alert the author sleeping at his desk,
The curate and the mower in the fields.
A bucket fills and overflows, abandoned
To blacken the stones of a whitewashed yard.
In the brown upper rooms there are women
Attending to letters. We are not permitted
To stand at their shoulders and may not
Determine the date, but the subject
Is things going on as they must, the summer
Still adding fresh months to itself, and the way
You'd never guess by simply looking round.

How easy to know where we stand, within sight
Of the back-to-front fingerpost, certain
That commandeered railings still rust
In the sidings, that somewhere up there
In the ferns is what looks like a gate
But is really a lock on the gelid
Forgotten canal, that its waters retain
All their monochrome heat and exist
For the drenching of constables.
O Mr Porter, the convicts are coming,
Ineptly, their suits full of arrows,
Over the dismal, bunkered levels,
Still sawing their irons and shouting.

It's midnight. On schedule, the ghost train
Is failing the bend by the claypits,
And stiff with old service revolvers,
Unsleeping on hard wooden chairs—
The price of this unnecessary trip—
We stare at the waiting-room fireplace and know
That the corpse in its bundle of coats
Will awake and the door be flung open
When Hammerpond enters, no longer a tramp,
To deliver the long explanation
Whose end we will miss when the radio coughs
And announces that all roads are flooded,
The sovereign's in Canada, Hitler in Brighton,
And no one will leave here tonight.

THIRTEEN AND COUNTING

Nothing political happens to them,
The thirteen girls who ascended the pile.
Up in Essex they care for their animals,
Honour the Queen and look forward to camp,
Which is flags of all nations and singing,
Night walks in the woods and First Aid
With a strong cup of tea. In the albums
Are photos the parents intend to raise laughter
In children of children: the girls on the pile
Wearing hard-hats, excited and formal
And raising their hands to enrol.
Their hair and their shoes are not burning.
The weather was cold but the day a success,
And when they were screened, not a tick.
Three days when it leaked were quite different,
As painstaking records confirm,
So they didn't need suits or shoes, even.
Their Captain, their parents, had no need to know,
And still less the thirteen, of the troublesome
Spot which occurred on the pile cap floor.
What it is to be young, in the Guides,
Before politics, thirteen and counting.

BOUNDARY BEACH

Invalids, perverts, and chambermaids born to be duped,
And those characters never awarded a name
Who must pass just before and just after the moment
And never be wiser: they have been here.

And the bad men themselves, stepping on to the grass
With a hum of the sexual magnet, were here.
The bad women whom cash and contempt had enraged
Were seen waiting, the sisters of Ruth, to be hanged

All along the blue border of Sussex and England
Where everything stops, even money, on Boundary Beach.
They arrived in their fugitive tenses, like art.
One would ladder a stocking, another count change

In the torment of not-quite-enough, and the third be on hand
With a wallet to match the occasion, a car
And the promise of waking up changed. They were English
And liked a good murder, the thrill of comeuppance

Achieved in the shelter behind the hotel. The detectives
Were born to the trade. Their exhaustion and fury
Would fill the slow shoes of the law, put its questions
From Volks to the fringes of Shoreham and go

Through the head-scratching, half-sipping migraine,
The grey, overheated minuteness that led
To the tawdry perception—a ticket, a stain—and then on
To a room by the A23 and the motive. Imagine them

Coming downstairs with the knowledge,
The windowless corridors left with their keyholes
And Do Not Disturbs, their adulteries, there at the death
While a constable sat in the kitchen, his collar undone,

As he wiped his moustache free of mustard
And offered his view to a maid and the boots
Who would read the same evening a fuller report
And glance out at the darkness before turning in,

In a hundred hotels that claim views of the sea,
Where the sleepless are counting the waves,
All along the blue border of Sussex and England,
Where everything stops, even money, on Boundary Beach.

THE BRIGHTON GOODBYE

This is the place we imagine we live,
Where the land slowly stops,
Among streets where the sea is implied
In white walls and expectant top windows
Left open for signals offshore.
The air is as bright as the harbour at noon
In the heat that can turn even cops into punters
And which we inhabit like natives of summer,
As if we had known it must come.
Now everyone seems to be leaving:
The bar-room will empty tonight
And be shuttered tomorrow,
A capsule of posters and still-sticky tables,
Its music absorbed into smoke.
The girl in the shop buying fruit
Has her mind on a schedule,
Her brown skin important with travel.
The old have prepared for a lifetime,
And now as they sit on their doorsteps
And wait to be told or collected
They cancel the hours with freesheets
Whose Gilbert and Sullivans, dogtracks
And fifteen quid bargains are clues
To a culture they've never known
Time or the passion to learn.
It is suddenly late. The afternoon yawns
And continues. A lean-to of shade
In a sunken backyard is the colour
Of Indian ink at the moment
The ferry swings out of the bay,
When the sea has no need to be local
And shows you the colour it keeps for itself,
Which you look at with terror and love.

2

AT THE WELLGATE

Their speechless cries left hanging in the cold
As human fog, as auditory stench,
The boreal flâneurs donate their stains
And thick cirrhotic sherries to the bench
Outside the precinct where they're not allowed,
And finding they've no stories left to tell
And thus no purchase on the Christmas crowd,
Descend by means of manholes into Hell.

Which in their case is arctic and unmapped,
Its every inch the coiling thick of it,
As if the Piranesi of the tubes
Had framed a labyrinth of frozen shit,
In which they wander howling and rehearse
The notion that elsewhere could still be worse.

MISSION IMPOSSIBLE

for Bob Hughes

The Corps of The Royal Flying Headers
Dundee Battalion (motto: Get Tae Fuck)
Has once more secured its objectives.

Forbidden in every conceivable boozer
Again, the survivors identify
What must be wreckage and what might be them,

And following one-handed Phal/Vindaloo
Plus the ritual piss in a doorway agree
To go thirds on the taxi. There follow

Some savage exchanges in cab-queues
With coatless and possibly pantless
Young ladies who though they themselves

Have been lately expelled from improbable dives
Are nonetheless frank in their disinclination
To come for a quick one in Fintry.

It's snowing. The drivers are taking
No prisoners, not even the damp-trousered wounded.
And this, the men tell you, retreating

In fairly good order up Hilltown, is This,
Which the averagely slaughtered would not understand,
A civil war that thankless volunteers

Must wage by night from street to street
For pride and the arcane insignia
Of groin and headbutt, glass and bar.

DUNDEE HEATWAVE

The rotundas of the mercantile retired
Glint with speculation. Telescopes are aimed
Along horizons sudden heat has blurred,
Where Fife habitually stands.
Low steamers slide beneath the bridge
For the remote interiors. Northern tropics
Sweat in the mind's eye and offer
Their opals and foot-rot and concubines
Round the next bend, or the next,
Or wherever young Hawkins and Hannay
Awake in their hammocks, alert
To the sshh of a dog-end in water.
That was the promise, think brittle old men,
Recapping the lenses and gingerly going
Downstairs to the papers and still afternoons
In the cool of their money, to study
The movements of shadows that reach
For their final disposal, the perfect just-so
That accounts for the rest, like a moral.
That was the promise, of stepping from shore
At the foot of the page, the beginning.

CAPTAIN JANUARY

On the backstreets of Occupied Europe
One day, one unspecified year, it is winter.
The snow is hard-packed on the cobbles.
The gates of the courtyards are shut
And the water has set in the bowls
And the towels have stiffened beside them
At windows whose curtains are drawn. Remotely
A motorbike roars at the silence.
It means there are marshlands and fields
Where the telegraph wires sing out of the East,
That farm-buildings stand among willows
Grown waist-deep in ice,
That the sound of a kick-started motorbike
Makes a room stare at itself.
Those who might liberate do not exist
As we might in that place. I might reach
For your hand on the oilcloth and hold it
And listen for sound that was no longer there
To remind me of who I had been
When we might for example
Have kicked off our shoes, gone upstairs
And considered our actions there private.
Jack One, Jack Two, and all the secret suit,
You're needed. Captain January rides,
And his sound is that bronchial utterance
Out on the roads, going somewhere.

PERSISTENCE

In the maintenance corridor somewhere below
Someone is dragging a bucket of dried-up cement.

You could hear it snag on the runners in doorways
And the private *thok* as it comes upright.

The clock and cloudy weather,
The low volume of afternoon traffic,

The city editions arriving on newsagents' counters
All give their consent. Things continue,

Among them this task, whose inception
Has not been made clear; and its agent,

Who wrestles his bucket to stand on a desk
In a windowless room at the corridor's end,

Likewise continues. He takes out the slip
From his overall pocket and offers the use of his biro

To air and the view of Caithness on the calendar
Thoughtfully placed on the opposite wall.

FISHING

On the edge of the light from the tea-bar
Where lorries bound westwards pull in,
With the hood of his anorak up
In the darkening drizzle,
He waits for the river to fill.
His friends are on fire with Samurai scotch,
Their window-cleaning ventures failed
Like stolen paint and threats and promises.
But he was always patient as the dead.
You could restock the Army and Navy
With wellingtons found in the reedbeds
And sell back Ninewells its syringes.
The water, he sees, is a warehouse.
And then there's the human dimension,
The surplus the tide has to try and unload,
Who must still, in this unmythological age,
Come ashore and pay money to do it.

NOTES ON THE USE OF THE LIBRARY (BASEMENT ANNEXE)

For John Bagnall

1

The Principal's other edition of Q,
Scott by the truckload, and Fredegond Shove,
Manuals instructing the dead how to do
What they no longer can with the Torments of Love
Mistaken assumptions concerning The Race,
Twelve-volume memoirs of footling campaigns,
Discredited physics, the Criminal Face,
Confessions of clerics who blew out their brains,
Laws and Geographies (utterly changed),
Travellers' journals that led up the creek,
The verbose, the inept and the clearly deranged,
The languages no one has bothered to speak,
And journals of subjects that do not exist:
What better excuse to go out and get pissed?

2

Here is the body of knowledge at rest
In its cavernous basement of headachy light.
Here lie the unread who were boring at best,
And guarding the door is their acolyte,
Grim Miss McNair with her own magazine,
Which is not the extinct *Vulcanologique*
But her sister's new copy of *Harpers and Queen*,
From which she looks up to forbid you to speak.

She means it. Their case is officially shut.
Their posthumous function is solely to warn,
via silence and odour and pages not cut,
That they, like their authors, should not have been born,
And hers to ensure, with her book-burner's glare,
That no one will add to what's already there.

IN RESIDENCE: A WORST CASE VIEW

This is the flat with its absence of curtains.
This is the bed which does not fit.
Here is your view of the silvery Tay:
Now what are you going to do with it?

Here are the tenements out at the back,
Die Dundee *alte Sächlichkeit*.
Here are the bins where the carryouts go
And here is the dead of the Calvinist night.

Here is the bandstand, here the wee bus,
Here is the railbridge. That is a train.
And here is the wind like God's right hook,
And his uppercut, and the pissing-down rain.

Next is the campus, brimstone-grim,
In which is the Dept., in which sits the Prof.,
Eyeing you narrowly, taking you in,
Not liking the sound of that smoker's cough.

And that was the tremor of inner dissent—
The colleague convinced he was robbed of the Chair
And his friend who agrees and the spy who does not:
Now button your lip and get out of there.

This is your office. That is your desk.
Here are your view and your paperclips—
Manage the first week, feeling your way,
Making a necklace and watching the ships.

Here is the notice you put on the board,
And these are the students beating a path
From their latest adventures in learning to spell
To a common obsession with Sylvia Plath.

Soon there are Tuesdays, long afternoons,
Letting them tell you what's good about Pound.
You smile and you nod and you offer them tea
And not one knows his arse from a hole in the ground.

And then there's the bloke who comes out for a drink,
Staring at legs while expounding Lacan.
It's a matter of time: will he get to the point
Before they arrive with the rubberized van?

Or else there are locals with serious pleasures—
Ten pints and ten whiskies and then an attack
Of the post-Flodden syndrome for which you're to blame.
You buy them another and leave by the back.

And this is the evening with nothing to do.
This is the evening when home's off the hook.
This is the evening for which you applied,
The leisure in which you should finish your book.

This is the point that permits no escape
From sitting in silence and getting it done,
Or sitting and screaming and fucking off out.
And this is the letter, and here is the gun.

To whom it concerns, I'm sorry I failed.
It seems I was utterly wrong to suppose
That by having the time I would finish the job,
Although I have put in the hours, God knows:

Hours of carryouts, hours of rain,
Hours of indolence mired in gloom—
I've tried and I've tried. I've even tried prose,
But the money's no good and I don't like the room.

BETWEENTIMES

There is an hour waiting in between.
In ruined districts, blue light waits.
Wrecking-yards and bar-rooms wait.
You can study the dust in the windows
Of incomprehensible premises, guess
At the null carborundum, clamped to its bench,
At all the further streets these streets conceal—

Their distant interiors, pillars of air
Under skylights where somebody stood
For a smoke, at the pinups entombed
In the necropolis of lockers, at calendars,
Invoices, indents of chair-legs in floorboards,
At tab-ends in cold-stores, and voices you know
Are not talking tonight after work.

No clockface admits it, the in-between hour.
Over the road an old barmaid of thirty
Rehearses a spin on high white heels
And supplies, unrequested, a pint
To the old man re-reading the paper.
You'd think they had built this around him,
Brick and varnish, optics, disappointment.

This is how waiting turns into a life,
In the hour it seems would explain
If the mind could forget what it thinks
About failure and history and money, and watch
How aesthetics takes leave of its senses,
In love with the facts of the matter,
The blue light and derelict happiness.

3

HMS GLASSHOUSE

At this hour the park offers only
A steam-heated acre of glass,
A sign in fresh hardboard, and somewhere
To wait while appearing to act.

We step inside its vaulted heat,
Its bleared below-decks light. We taste
Its air of rot and counter-rot, attend
Its vegetable politics, and watch

As plants with webbed and shellacked hands
Swarm up the stanchions, offering
The universal shrug of making do,
Like the teenagers painting the catwalks,

Who might once have painted the hulls
Of the frigates and merchantmen sent
To secure the Malvinas for mutton.
Their status as national assets has lapsed

And the registers cancel their names:
They are guilty again, as am I, as are you,
As the glasshouse sweats on
Like the *Unterseeboot* of the state

With its periscope down, its orders sealed,
Its routine a deliberate torpor.
We wake in the very same place
With the curious notion that fish

Have been crowding the glass to peer in
At the items preserved for the voyage—
Cast-iron and Pilkingtons' finest,
Odd volumes of Oakeshott and Scruton

To kill off the time, in an atmosphere
Soon to be poison. Let's make our inspection
On tiptoe, and listen for cracks
In case one of us throws the first stone.

COLD

They have opened the holds of the trawlers,
The dozen not sold off or scrapped,
And cold has been released into the city.
These are the businesslike highlights of cold.
We're talking Kelvin: this is cold
From the North of the North, in a Russian abundance

Renewed at each corner, as now
When the bus station comes into view,
With its arc lights resharpened by ice
At the point of departure,
Green girders, a warehouse of gallows,
And night like a jeweller's pad.

Such difficult venues are magnets
For those who have nowhere to travel.
They come as if promised a ride way back
And having been abandoned once
Can only circle and return, their pleas unheard,
Grown used to the contempt of the authentic.

The place is a test. Who stays too long?
The man lying prone with his history of bags
Who's just failed in a desperate attempt
To reclaim an old selfhood by vaulting the railings
Provides an example. Forget him.
A cabbie could show you a hundred

In all the right places—the end of the pier,
In the doorways of missions attempting their names,
On bombsites or dancing their solos
Across the new precincts, the comics
Not even their mothers would book,
Too gone to know they'll freeze tonight

On Blanket Row and Beggar Lane, marooned
On the spit where the stream from the city
Goes under the river, unquenchably roaring
Its terrible promise, the one they can almost remember
From childhood, an atlas of oceans
That sounds like a mouthful of stones.

DRY SAILORS

Becalmed at this table next door to a river
No one these days navigates,
The water-clerks, white suits in pawn,
Have boarded the island of restaurants
To sail theoretical oceans.

The White Star, the Black Star and Ellerman Wilson—
Their funnels behind the back roofs
Of an atlas of cities,
Those Grimshaws of rigging and smoke
In which all the best streets come to nothing—

We know them the way we know Conrad,
By longing for water but having to read it,
The lifetime of manuscripts found in the bottle.
So often we finish the night
In the glamour of not setting out—

Foam dried at the rim of the glass,
Fog rinsing the cobbles.
But oceans depart at the corner:
We've known it since first we imagined the tides
From their half column-inch in the sports page

Spread out when the kitchen was mopped,
Since we climbed to the landing as if from up there
We might see what we heard of the sirens
Becoming the distance. Remember the estuary
Turning for home, and the charts we agreed

Would grow dark as the bed fell away . . .
Then the officer takes out his pen and his diary,
His copy of *Within the Tides*,
To write up the extracts his grandson will find:
Which is always the way it begins,

With edifying copperplate,
The figure bent beneath the lamp, and from below
M'Andrew's hymn vibrating every surface
With the promise of a storm, while under that
Lie multiplying fathoms,

The traffic of monsters and hearsay that tells us
Where *Nautilus* breaches the icecap,
That Nemo discovers the fiction of Verne
And the coffin of Queequeg
Is found to contain exegesis more precious

Than anything Ishmael could offer,
Who, let us speak frankly,
Must suffer from too much involvement, neglecting
To number the barnacles clamped to the vanishing hull
Or to notice the albatross

Sighing its way to the 'distant speck'
Which might after all have been Hudson
Or Franklin or Sinbad or one of a thousand . . .
Or maybe, the hope we're too old to admit,
Just a skiff on the rim of the maelstrom

In which every text will be sunk,
Where as we spin the compass we can see
Beyond the reach of curse and commentary
An ocean quite empty of all but the weather
And us, and the log we shall quickly forget.

ON THE PISS

They want it right now, do the serious drinkers.
The thirty-year men with no surnames
Go straight to the throat of the matter
For urgent interior drenching and burning
To keep the toxicity up to the mark,
Scum rimming the bath of the body.
They used to be somewhere quite different,
At sea or in jail or pretending to settle
On spartan estates and be married.
They've no sense of humour about it,
No photographs either. One day at a time,
They imply, looking round from the bar
As if something tremendous they've always been offered
Turns out to be merely the carpet unzipping
To vomit its cellar of demons.
No matter. There's more where that came from,
A holdall of shirts and the racing on loud,
The face slapped with alcohol, mouthwash
Reminding the tongue what it wants.
Mirror-balls, mirror-tiles. Where it is brittle
And carpets are crusty, in submarine discos
Now boasting a brand new selection of towels to tread on
And doorbolts designed to rip sleeves and break nails,
The walls good for slumping, no paper,
They find themselves seated in violent laughter
With likeminded women—girls until looked at,
Whose heels keep on breaking, who cannot stop
Screeching or crying or finding themselves being hit
For misplaced and forgotten adventures
With other such mateys because it was Christmas
Or someone had won the St Leger. Their lordships
Keep grazing their cheeks with their watches
While wiping the sweat from their pleasure.
Their voices belong with the shit-stained ceramics
And doors riven off. They deliver uncatchable
Howls from the corridor, make styluses jump
Like a warning to someone not there
Who might suddenly turn into you.
They are seen in the parched red interiors
Long after closing, their hands up the skirts

Of unconscious companions, unconscious themselves
With their mouths still at work, wanting more.
They are ready for anywhere tiled and awash
To abrade and contuse in, for rooms where the furniture
Goes to be smashed or to burst into flame,
And their kids have been lied to and stolen
In some other city they will not go into,
For reasons that never were your bastard business.

FROM THE WHALEBONE

These evenings I step from the Whalebone
At time-on-your-beer for a piss out the back,
And then stand in the mixture of moonlight and sodium,
Waiting and taking it in.
The powdery blue of high summer
Refires the bricks red and black.
There are gaps in the traffic
Where water runs through. And I'm old.
The fifty-year mild-drinking errand
Has carried me this way most nights,
Over ironclad bridges, past tanneries,
Headstones, the grey river glimpsed
As it roars to itself at the bend
To be done with its name in a mile,
And down at the swingbridge the railway sets off
To its vanishing-point, where the houses
And streetlamps run out and the last bus
Turns back. You get all that from here.
It was only the meantime, this amateur city
That never believed where it was.
Behind it the secretive flatlands
Are closed for the night, for the century,
Minding a dialect, a closeness to water
That water is bearing away.
I shall sit on a fly-haunted coach
While it shrugs off the hedgerows and lingers
At shelters where nobody gets on or off,
And then walk the last bit to be sure how it stands,
Grey-green, coming in, the horizon in place
And the atlas beyond it unopened.

WORKING ON THE RAILWAY

You are trying to work but you sit
With the wrong book entirely: *Lost Railways of England*,
Whose dust of the forties, the fifties,
Is making you sneeze. When you just have a look
At the picture of steam as it swallows the bridge
At Botanic, you're going. Then Stepney, Stoneferry
And Wilmington. Flatlands. The vanished resorts
Where the girls run down into the water
Like spies with a half-hour free,
Then back to the baker's, the nightschool,
The sombre saloon of the Station Hotel.
Past the window the *Montague Finnegan*
Pulls away north, and the soldiers are crowding
The corridors, wishing that girls were laid on
To be waving farewell, like the future,
A bed you need never get out of.
From there you could grasp it, the railway,
The sea creaming in at the piers,
And just round the corner the carriages stand
In the first of the heat, with their headachy air
Full of dustmotes, their pictures of elsewhere:
An hour of silence that seems to be England,
The life it was offered once only,
Its trivial, infinite distances—
Promises, promises. Write it all down.

ON THE LINE

I'm awaiting the right afternoon
When there's nothing to read and no work,
When I'll find I've gone out for tobacco
And never come back. I'll step over
The line that divides my own place
From the one where the map has no answers.

Not even the nineteenth century managed
To fill in the gaps. The red factories stand
With their decoys of steam, on short time
In a soup made of old grass and water,
And looking is never enough to reveal
What comes after. It might still be houses,

Or schools left in acres of brickdust,
The sheds of a last-ditch allotment
Or simply the first line of hawthorns
That marks the true edge of the city.
I aim where I know I won't reach—
I'm describing a circle whose grain-wharves

And cakemills will slide into view
At the end of each tilt of the compass.
I'll follow the rails through a hangar of dust
And come out on the edge of the evening
Beside the brick path to the swingbridge
Where one light is burning and nobody's home,

And though twenty years' growth
Says the line is abandoned, I'll still
Put my ear to the track, and a penny, then sit
On the bankside, on cinders not cold enough yet
To undo the conviction that if I go up
And look hard the far signal will change.

SERIOUS

Let us be serious now, says the teacher,
Inserting a pause in the hot afternoon
As she steeples her fingers and waits.

It's hard not to look at the snow
That prolongs the blue end of the day,
Not to think of it gathered

In alleys and gardens across the flat town
For a footprint, but this is Miss Garvin
And those are her fingers,

And though her long nails are a vanity
None of the sisters approves,
She speaks as they speak, for a power

That means us to answer the serious question
We have not been asked, that we cannot imagine
Or fail to be wrong in attempting:

Therefore we are serious now, as we wonder
Who might be the shameful example
To prove the unspecified point.

It may lie in the fork of a crocus
Or bury a jamjar left out on the step,
Or fall in its passion for detail

On two unburnt coals in the grate,
But the snow cannot help or survive
In the heat of the serious moment,

The void of all content
Where something, as ever, is wrong.
Across the yard the boilers roar.

Good children, we long to be serious well,
To multiply the word on slates,
To raise our voices in its name

And wear its ash with modesty.
We slip our hands behind the pipes
And turn them into gloves of pain.

NAUGHTY RON

When Naughty Ron said middle age
Began at forty-five,
We grinned, convinced he must be mad
To choose to stay alive,

Considering that at thirty-nine
And threatened with the nick,
He still found little boys inclined
To make him raise his stick.

Poor bastard. If he's still around,
I think I see his room:
Its 'discs', its photos of the Fourth,
Part opera house, part tomb,

With sixty growing plausible
And after that, who knows?
But not much chance of supple lads
To smile and touch their toes.

Conscription took him to the Med
And showed him what was what,
An exiled bookish elegance,
But not how it was got,

So time became a preface
To his coming into style:
He thought—and it's his epitaph—
Of teaching for a while,

And that was where we left him,
Five minutes from the sack,
Dictating notes on *Mansfield Park*
While we sat near the back

Examining our pity
Like a warning from the bank:
Imagine life with nothing left
But Verdi and a wank.

BALLAD OF THE LIT AND PHIL

When I went in that afternoon
With work that must be done
I should have left the books at home
And fetched a scatter-gun.

For all that things seemed quiet
In the varnished vestibule
The maze of galleries beyond
Was given to misrule,

And the enemies of silence
Were waiting in the stacks
And at a given signal
Commenced with their attacks:

To start with, just the graveyard cough,
The snigger and the snerk,
Then someone bawling, *Mustn't chat —
I've come in here to work*,

But somehow taking ages
To get the one thing said,
And hovering, and fingering
The Listener instead.

Thus the hours screamed away,
Distracted into dust,
But there were deadlines to be met —
I worked because I must.

I bowed my head and thumbed my ears
And damned if I'd give up.
One broke a chair. Another dropped
His top set in my cup,

And then the tea-lady came singing
And a-banging of her tray,
So clearly they could keep this up
The livelong bloody day.

Some others murdered violins
Somewhere beneath my feet

And blokes came in with spades and dug
The place up like a street.

But still I smiled and held my peace
And laboured down the page,
Until at last a silence fell
Like acid-drops of rage

Through which there came to sit with me
A leading local bore.
He told me how much parquet
Went to lay the library floor,

And how the old librarians
Would mix the morning's ink
And how much sugar Marat took
In what he liked to drink . . .

This last (alas) was interesting
And took me off my guard,
And glimpsing opportunity
He smiled and came in hard.

Please understand, this is a place
For people who pretend.
If someone tries to work in here
It drives us round the bend.

You think this is a library?
It's the temple of a sect
Whose article of faith
Is simple: Only disconnect.

We view ourselves as guardians
Of ignorance and sloth,
And no one stays a member here
Unless he swears to both.

Everywhere and always, friend,
Since language first was stored—
The mass of membership has been
A vast illiterate fraud.

Bodley, Austin, Pierpont Morgan,
Big UL and old BM—
Oh do you seriously think
That anybody reads in them?

And I dreamed a dream of libraries
Exactly as he said,
Repositories of indolence
Where nothing's ever read,

From Adelaide to Antioch,
From Zanzibar to Nome,
A vast deliberate vacancy,
An overarching dome.

The vision was the weariness
Ecclesiastes meant,
And suddenly I understood
The reason I'd been sent,

And why my hopes of wisdom
Were mere errors in the text.
O reader, can you understand
The thing that I did next?

Tenderly I took his head
And bashed it on the floor.
The next I knew, librarians
Were showing me the door.

They threw me out into the street
Where I am lying now.
They made me give my ticket back.
They said I made a row.

And now I'm banned from every
Bloody branch in town,
But I shall visit them by night
And burn the bastards down.

Oh weep for Alexandria,
That library-lacuna,
But left to me it would have turned
To ash a good deal sooner.

COMING HOME

These cold nights I catch it all clearly —
The terrace, its front rooms unlit
And kept only for coffins, the streetlamp
Grown cloudy with breath, where the children swing,
And the footprint set down in fresh snow
On a doorstep, as if by a template, still perfect.

A lightship intones that it too is a place,
Where the salt meets the fresh
And the tide in the estuary pauses
Before setting out with the fleet,
While the trawlermen sprint from their taxis,
Still dressed up, still drunk and still broke.

Then there are white shores receding
And gone, with the last light still ghosting the eye
As the snow comes again and the complement
Enters the atlas you gave me, a place
Made of names which are cold and exciting to say
In the intimate arctic of almost-asleep.

I'm not meant to be out. I am catching my death,
But the first thing I want is a story.
Tonight I can live with the fact
That high in the darkness a crane waits
To build the infirmary you'll die in.
Tonight is reserved. I can always go back

To the moment I entered the world
To imagine its distance myself:
While the dead in the house with their teacups
Complain that the door is left open, I'll wait
With the snow and the sirens, as long as it takes.

AN ORDINARY EVENING IN NEW HOLDERNESS

Suppose that the summer is ending tonight,
As by treaty, that August surrenders the town
On the ultimate stroke of its name.

The heat will run down like a battery,
Spending itself through the windows and flagstones
As far as the sea, where its pulse can be felt

In the sand that keeps drinking the surf
As though to continue would draw the far cities
To rim the horizon with light.

In imperial times there were lamps at this pond,
But this evening a matchflare suffices
To bring the air closer and show us

The remnants of weddings and carryouts
Called to the thick of it,
Propped in the mouths of the shelters

Or sitting out under the limes
At whose edges rooms open on rooms
And then air, and the space above trees

Is domestic, as if out of sight
Must be somebody sitting and smoking,
Not bothered, not needing to talk.

A CORRIDOR

for Henry Katz

The shoulder-high tiles in municipal green,
The brown walls, the bare lavatorial floor
Which is always about to be damp,
The heavy swing doors we shall not
Be exploring today; the long view
We are taking this late afternoon—
Whose end is obscure
With November indoors, it would seem—
In the fifties, when we were much smaller
And quickly impressed by the minor displays
Of the State which would aim us
From cradle to grave, you remember:
All this we inherit, a corridor
Built by the Irish for God and the Queen.

We trap our germs in handkerchiefs.
We do not spit when on the bus.
Out where the city once turned into fields
Are prefabs growing permanent:
To each its patch of grass, from each a vote.
And here where the corridor turns in a fury of echoes
My father is leaving the party for nowhere,
The intimate cell where the struggle is waged
Over doughnuts in Lyons, the afternoons hung
With sheets of Players, the talk of betrayal.
It's what lies before us when we are too old
To be sure—which was never his problem.
The problems he had were the world
And his terrible spelling, I'm told.
They have rolled up the speeches, the grass from the park
After Mayday and stored them in here.

Behind the baize door a committee
Is handing the scholarships out—
A régime of deaf butchers and bandit accountants
Rewarded for lifetimes of ignorance,
Waiting to get our names wrong.
In the clinic a sinister lady

Will study my feet and insist
I can reach the trapeze.
My grandfather wheels a dead man
To the morgue for a pittance
And votes the wrong way as a duty
To something the next war was meant to disprove.
We vanish to Mafeking, Simla,
The moth-eaten middle of Ireland
Where Marx is a nightmare
That God isn't having
And people like us are a gleam of prolepsis
In somebody's eye—the well-meaning
Impotent heirs to the corridor,
Pacing it out past the dinner-money's chink,
Cries from the dentist and telephones nobody answers,
Incompetent dreaming, corrupt and forgetful,
The cellars of pamphlets for futures
That nobody lived. This is ours. Keep walking.

TO THE UNKNOWN GOD OF HULL AND HOLDERNESS

In memory of Frank Redpath

'For that the God abounds in examples'

God of blind corners and defunct commercial premises,
God of altered streetnames and of lost amenities,
God of the shut bath-house and the dry swimming pool,
   the leased-out playing field, the partial view
   to what lies past the railway land,
Go with us.

God of the back way,
God of Felix Marsden's route,
God of the Bear and Top House and Full Measure,
God of the windy bus-shelter and the flapping hoarding,
God of the hole in the fence, of the cindery feet of
   embankments,
God of the flattened penny,
Go with us.

God of rumoured ships and proven stenches,
God of the Woolsheds and the sidings,
God of square scorches in grassland,
God of the marquee's imprint and of yellow grass,
God of the infilled drainsite,
God of the windy corridors of board-schools and clinics,
God of sheds wherever they may lean,
God of the in-between district neither Stoneferry nor Stepney,
God of the district not served by the buses,
Go with us.

God of gutted signal-boxes,
God of aimless Sunday walks,
God of the unrestored graveyards,
God of fallen angels under leafmould,
God of flooded tenfoots,
God of the back bar's spongy, sodden seats,
God of the not-yet afforested quarry,
God of the corrugated echo of the whiteworks,
God of the turntable and adjacent sewage farm,

God of the tracks that divide so that one will be always
    unknown,
God of the green MAIL and of Queen of the South and
    Stenhousmuir
God of the teatimes of 1958,
Go with us.

God of dead aerodromes,
God of seamed asphalt,
God of unbearable Sundays that taught us to wait,
God of pits in the clay where the water climbed up,
God of the slow deaths of mattresses split on the waste patch,
God of preposterous stained-glass heraldic imaginings left in the
    house of the barmy Lord Mayor,
God who has room for the nuns in the day and by night for the
    carved wooden heads of Silenus that stared from
    the fireplace,
Go with us.

God of the Third Division North,
God of Chilton, Wagstaff, Houghton, Butler,
Though not (alas) of Henderson,
God of the drains and bombsites,
God of the fathers on forty a day,
God of comics and encyclopaedias,
God of Sunk Island, stalled ferries,
God of the sea and its fine disregard of established geography,
God of school-dinners and Blackjacks,
God of the snowball and halfbrick,
Go with us.

God of the upper back window, the privet, the dark afternoon,
God of the dock-leaf and groundsel,
God of white dog-turds not found since the fifties,
God of the orchard, the sickle, the fountain,
God of all summers, all boredom,
God of the book and the start of the trouble,
God of white paper, of iambs and dactyls,
God who gives all but the transitive verb,
Now and in the hour of bafflement
Before your works and what they mean,
Be hidden and persist.

AFTER LAFORGUE

In memory of Martin Bell

I have put a blockade on high-mindedness.
All night, through dawn and dead mid-morning,
Rain is playing rimshots on a bucket in the yard.
The weatherman tells me that winter comes on
As if he'd invented it. Fuck him.

Fuck sunshine and airports and pleasure.
Wind is deadheading the lilacs inland.
You know what this means. I could sing.
The weekend sailors deal the cards and swear.
The Channel is closed. This is good.

In the sopping, padlocked, broad-leaved shade of money
Desperate lunches are cooking
In time for the afternoon furies and sudden
Divorces of debt from the means of production.
Good also. These counties are closed.

Myself, I imagine the north in its drizzle,
Its vanished smoke, exploded chimneys: home
In bad weather to hills of long hospitals, home
To the regional problems of number, home
To sectarian strife in the precincts of Sheffield and Hartlepool,

Home from a world of late-liberal distraction
To rain and tenfoots clogged with leaves,
To the life's work of boredom and waiting,
The bus-station's just-closing teabar,
The icy, unpromising platforms of regional termini,

Home to dead docks and the vandalized showhouse.
Home for Mischief Night and Hallowe'en, their little tales,
When the benches (the sodden repose of old bastards in dog-
    smelling overcoats)
Vanish, when council employees dragged from the pub
Will be dragging the lake in the park,

Watching their footprints fill up
And hating those whose bastard lives
Are bastard lived indoors. Home,
As Sunday extends towards winter, a shivery kiss
In a doorway, *Songs of Praise*, last orders. Home.

Rain, with an angel's patience, remind me.
This is not the world of Miss Selfridge and Sock Shop,
Disposable income and lycra, illiterate hearsay
And just-scraping-in-after-Clearing to Business in Farnham.
This world is not Eastbourne. It has no opinions.

In this world it rains and the winter
Is always arriving—rebirth of TB
And *The Sporting Green* sunk to the drainbed.
Here is the stuff that gets left in the gaps
Between houses—ambitious settees in black frogskin

And minibars missing their castors, the catalogues
Turning to mush, the unnameable objects
That used to be something with knobs on,
And now they live here, by the siding, the fishhouse,
The building whose function is no longer known.

It is Londesborough Street with the roof gone—
That smell as the wallpaper goes, as it rains
On the landing, on pot dogs and photos
And ancient assumptions of upright servility.
Nothing is dry. The pillow-tick shivers

And water comes up through the scullery tiles
And as steam from the grate. There are funerals
Backed up the street for a mile
As the gravediggers wrestle with pumps and the vicar
Attempts to hang on to his accent.

Rain, with an angel's patience, teach me
The lesson of where I came in once again,
With icy vestibules and rubber pillows,
The dick-nurse, the wet-smelling ash in the yard
And the bleary top deck like a chest-ward.

Teach me the weather will always be worsening,
With the arctic fleet behind it—
The subject of talk in the shop, at the corner,
Or thought of when stepping out into the yard
To the sirens of factories and pilot-boats,

There like a promise, the minute at nightfall
When rain turns to snow and is winter.

OXFORD POETS

Fleur Adcock

Moniza Alvi

Kamau Brathwaite

Joseph Brodsky

Basil Bunting

Tessa Rose Chester

Daniela Crăsnaru

Michael Donaghy

Keith Douglas

D. J. Enright

Roy Fisher

Ida Affleck Graves

Ivor Gurney

David Harsent

Gwen Harwood

Anthony Hecht

Zbigniew Herbert

Tobias Hill

Thomas Kinsella

Brad Leithauser

Derek Mahon

Jamie McKendrick

Sean O'Brien

Alice Oswald

Peter Porter

Craig Raine

Zsuzsa Rakovszky

Christopher Reid

Stephen Romer

Eva Salzman

Carole Satyamurti

Peter Scupham

Jo Shapcott

Penelope Shuttle

Goran Simić

Anne Stevenson

George Szirtes

Grete Tartler

Edward Thomas

Charles Tomlinson

Marina Tsvetaeva

Chris Wallace Crabbe

Hugo Williams